It Could Still Be A Butterfly

WITHDRAWN

By Allan Fowler

Consultants

Robert L. Hillerich, Professor Emeritus,
Bowling Green State University, Bowling Green, Ohio;
Consultant, Pinellas County Schools, Florida

Lynne Kepler, Educational Consultant

Fay Robinson, Child Development Specialist

CHILDRENS PRESS®

CHICAGO

Design by Beth Herman Design Associates
Photo Research by Feldman & Associates, Inc.

Library of Congress Cataloging-in-Publication Data

Fowler, Allan.
    It could still be a butterfly / by Allan Fowler.
       p. cm. – (Rookie read-about science)
    ISBN 0-516-06028-7
    1. Butterflies–Juvenile literature. [1. Butterflies.]
  I. Title. II. Series.
QL544.2.F68   1994
595.78'9–dc20
                                     94-10470
                                            CIP
                                            AC

Which is the prettiest insect? Many people would say it's the butterfly.

Butterflies usually fly
during the daytime.
They may rest on flowers
with their wings open . . .

or they may fold their
wings upward and together.

If you see an insect that looks like a butterfly, but is flying at night . . . or is resting with its wings spread flat, like this . . . then it is probably a moth, not a butterfly.

A butterfly can be any one of 80,000 different species, or kinds — and still be a butterfly. The Painted Lady is a very pretty and very common butterfly.

Some butterflies are named after their color — such as the Silvery Blue.

Not all butterflies are as brightly colored as Painted Ladies and Silvery Blues.

A butterfly can be a dull brownish color with black spots, like the Satyr — and still be a butterfly.

It can measure as much as 8 inches from the tip of one wing to the tip of the other wing — and still be a butterfly. That is bigger than this page!

Butterflies that big are found only where the weather is warm all year round.

The largest butterfly you are likely to see in North America is the Swallowtail.

Butterflies have two pairs of
scaly wings. They have six
legs, as all adult insects do.

That long, coiled tube you see
is the butterfly's mouth. To eat,
the butterfly uncoils the tube
and sips the sweet juice from
flowers through it. The juice
is called nectar.

Some butterflies escape their enemies because their colors make them hard to see.

Some butterflies, such as
the Monarch, taste bad —
and birds won't eat them.

Every autumn, the
Monarch butterflies fly
south from Canada or the
northern United States.
This is called migration.

They fly to warm places
in southern California or
Mexico. They spend the
winter there.

Thousands of Monarchs may
rest in a single tree. They look
like fluttering orange flowers.

In the spring, they fly back north. They lay eggs and begin a new cycle of life.

Every butterfly goes through four stages in its life. And the butterfly looks completely different at each stage.

The butterfly begins
as an egg.

The egg hatches, and
a caterpillar crawls out.

The tiny caterpillar eats
until it becomes big and fat.

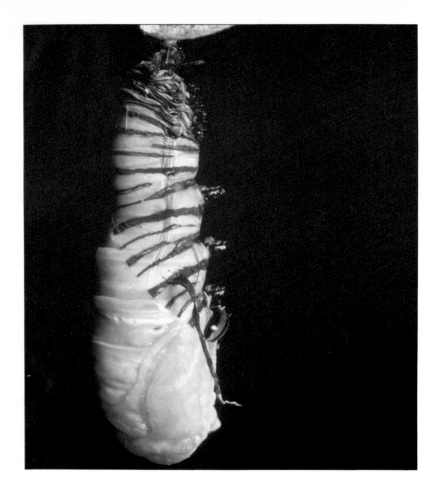

Then it sheds its skin and
becomes a chrysalis.

The chrysalis doesn't
move, but inside, the
insect keeps changing.

Soon, the chrysalis breaks open. A beautiful butterfly climbs out —

and flies away.

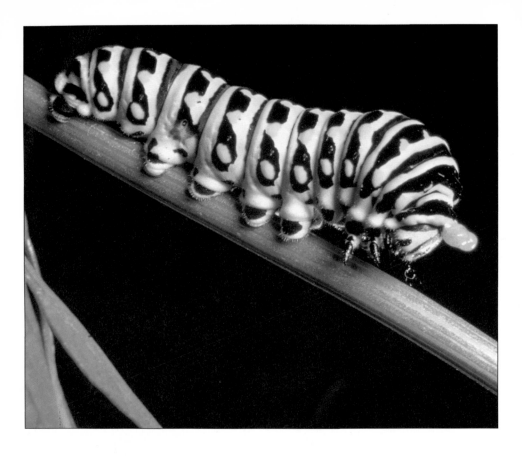

A creeping caterpillar
may not seem very
beautiful or graceful.

But remember, though it's just a caterpillar now . . . it could still be a butterfly someday.

Words You Know

egg

chrysalis

caterpillar

Monarch butterfly

Painted Lady

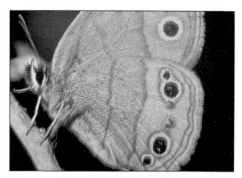

Satyr butterfly

Swallowtail

moth

Index

About the Author

Allan Fowler is a free-lance writer with a background in advertising. Born in New York, he lives in Chicago now and enjoys traveling.

Photo Credits

SuperStock International, Inc. – Cover, ©H. Lanks, 16; ©M. Keller, 27

Valan – ©Alan Wilkinson, 4; ©John Fowler, 5, 9, 13, 17, 21, 28, 30 (top left), 31 (top & bottom left); ©Pam E. Hickman, 7, 15, 24, 31 (bottom right); ©J.R. Page, 8, 31 (center left); ©Aubrey Lang, 19; ©Pat Louis, 22; ©John Mitchell, 23, 29, 30 (bottom)

Visuals Unlimited – ©Bill Beatty, 11, 31 (center right); ©D. Cavagnoro, 14; ©William J. Weber, 25, 30 (top right); ©Dan Kline, 26

COVER: Eastern Black Swallowtail